Drug Addiction Recovery Skills with No Relapse

Bergeron T. Baker

Copyright ©

Table of Contents

Introduction

Addiction is a complex and multifaceted disease that affects millions of individuals worldwide, regardless of age, gender, or socioeconomic status.

It not only impacts the individual struggling with addiction but also their loved ones, communities, and society as a whole. However, amidst the darkness of addiction, there is hope for recovery.

In these pages, you will find a wealth of practical strategies, evidence-based techniques, and empowering insights to support you on your path to sobriety.

Whether you are just beginning your recovery journey or have been on this road for some time, this book offers a roadmap to navigate the challenges, overcome obstacles, and build a life filled with purpose, meaning, and fulfillment.

Our approach is grounded in the understanding that true recovery goes beyond mere abstinence from drugs.

It involves a holistic transformation of mind, body, and spirit. Through a combination of self-reflection, education, skill-building, and support, you will learn to cultivate the resilience, inner strength, and coping mechanisms necessary to thrive in recovery.

Each chapter is designed to address key aspects of the recovery process, from understanding the science of addiction to developing relapse prevention strategies, from practicing mindfulness and self-compassion to rebuilding relationships and finding meaning in life beyond addiction.

It's important to acknowledge that the journey to recovery is not always linear. There may be setbacks, challenges, and moments of doubt along the way.

However, by arming yourself with the knowledge, skills, and resources contained within these pages, you will be better equipped to navigate the ups and downs of recovery with grace, courage, and perseverance.

Remember, you are not alone in this journey. There is a vast community of individuals, professionals, and support networks ready to walk alongside you and offer guidance, encouragement, and understanding. Together, we can break free from the chains of addiction and embrace a life of sobriety, purpose, and joy.

As you embark on this transformative journey, I invite you to approach it with an open mind, a compassionate heart, and a steadfast commitment to your own well-being.

May this book serve as a beacon of hope, inspiration, and empowerment as you take the first steps toward a brighter, drug-free future.

With courage and determination, let us embark on this journey of recovery together.

Drug Addiction and the Science Behind it

Drug addiction is a complex and chronic disease characterized by compulsive drug seeking, use, and relapse despite harmful consequences.

While addiction may start with voluntary drug use, continued use can lead to changes in the brain that compromise an individual's self-control and ability to resist intense impulses.

Understanding the science behind addiction is crucial in developing effective treatment and recovery strategies.

Neurobiology of Addiction:

At the core of addiction lies alterations in brain chemistry and circuitry. Drugs of abuse, whether they are opioids, stimulants, depressants, or others, hijack the brain's reward system, flooding it with neurotransmitters such as dopamine.

Dopamine is a neurotransmitter associated with pleasure and reward, and its release reinforces behaviors necessary for survival, such as eating and socializing.

When drugs are introduced, they artificially increase dopamine levels, producing intense feelings of pleasure or euphoria.

Over time, repeated drug use disrupts the brain's natural reward system, leading to a diminished response to normal stimuli and a reliance on drugs to feel pleasure. This phenomenon, known as tolerance, drives individuals to increase their drug dosage or frequency, perpetuating the cycle of addiction.

Brain Changes:

Long-term drug use also leads to profound changes in the brain's structure and function.

Chronic drug exposure alters the communication between neurons, rewiring neural circuits involved in motivation, memory, learning, and decision-making.

These changes contribute to the compulsive drug-seeking behaviors and cravings characteristic of addiction.

Additionally, drugs can impair the prefrontal cortex, the region of the brain responsible for executive functions such as impulse control, decision-making, and self-regulation. As a result, individuals struggling with addiction may have difficulty resisting drug cravings and making rational choices, even when they are aware of the negative consequences.

Psychological and Environmental Factors:

While the neurobiology of addiction provides insights into its underlying mechanisms, addiction is not solely a brain disorder.

Psychological, social, and environmental factors also play significant roles in the development and progression of addiction. Trauma, stress, mental health disorders, genetic predisposition, peer influence, and socioeconomic status can all contribute to vulnerability to addiction.

In summary, drug addiction is a multifaceted disease with biological, psychological, and social dimensions.

Understanding the science behind addiction helps to destigmatize the condition and underscores the importance of evidence-based treatments that address both the biological and psychosocial aspects of addiction.

By approaching addiction as a chronic medical condition, we can develop more effective prevention, intervention, and treatment strategies to support individuals on their journey to recovery.

The Road to Recovery

Acceptance and Commitment to Change

Acceptance and commitment to change are fundamental principles in the recovery journey from drug abuse.

These concepts, rooted in the field of cognitive-behavioral therapy (CBT) and mindfulness-based approaches, provide a solid foundation for individuals seeking to break free from the cycle of addiction.

Here's how acceptance and commitment to change can pave the way for recovery:

Acknowledging the Problem: Acceptance involves acknowledging the reality of one's drug abuse and its impact on various aspects of life, including physical health, relationships, finances, and emotional well-being. It requires honesty and self-awareness to recognize the harmful consequences of substance abuse without denial or defensiveness.

Embracing Responsibility: Acceptance also entails taking responsibility for one's actions and choices. Rather than blaming external factors or circumstances, individuals in recovery accept accountability for their behavior and recognize that they have the power to make positive changes in their lives.

Letting Go of Resistance: Resistance to change is a common barrier in addiction recovery. Acceptance involves letting go of resistance and embracing the process of change with openness and willingness. It requires surrendering to the present moment and being willing to explore new perspectives and possibilities.

Mindful Awareness: Mindfulness, a key component of acceptance-based approaches, involves nonjudgmental awareness of present-moment experiences.

By cultivating mindfulness skills, individuals in recovery can observe their thoughts, emotions, and cravings without reacting impulsively or being overwhelmed by them.

This allows for greater self-regulation and the ability to make conscious choices aligned with long-term goals.

Clarifying Values: Commitment to change involves clarifying one's values and aspirations for the future. By identifying what truly matters to them—such as health, family, career, spirituality, or personal growth—individuals can align their actions with their values and pursue a meaningful life beyond addiction.

Setting Goals: Once values are clarified, commitment to change entails setting specific, achievable goals that support those values.

These goals may include abstinence from drugs, improving physical health, rebuilding relationships, pursuing education or employment opportunities, or engaging in recreational activities.

Creating a Plan: Commitment to change requires developing a comprehensive plan for achieving one's goals. This may involve seeking professional help, attending support groups, participating in therapy, adopting healthier lifestyle habits, and implementing strategies for managing cravings and triggers.

Cultivating Resilience: Recovery from drug abuse is not a linear process, and setbacks are inevitable. Acceptance and commitment to change involve cultivating resilience and persistence in the face of challenges.

It requires learning from setbacks, adapting to obstacles, and staying focused on long-term recovery goals.

In summary, acceptance and commitment to change are powerful catalysts for recovery from drug abuse. By embracing acceptance, mindfulness, responsibility, values, and goals, you can pave the way for lasting transformation and reclaim their lives from the grip of addiction.

Setting Recovery Goals

Setting recovery goals is a crucial step in the journey toward overcoming drug abuse and building a fulfilling life in sobriety. Here's a comprehensive guide on how to set effective recovery goals:

Reflect on Your Values and Priorities:

Take some time to reflect on what matters most to you in life. Consider your values, aspirations, and long-term goals beyond drug abuse.

This could include aspects such as health, relationships, career, personal growth, and community involvement.

Identify Areas for Improvement:

Assess the various areas of your life that have been impacted by drug abuse, such as physical health, mental well-being, relationships, finances, and legal issues.

Identify specific areas where you would like to see improvement and where setting goals can help you make progress.

Make Your Goals Specific and Measurable:

Set clear, specific goals that are measurable and achievable. Instead of vague aspirations like "get healthier," set concrete objectives such as "exercise for 30 minutes three times a week" or "attend therapy sessions regularly."

Prioritize Your Goals:

Not all goals need to be tackled simultaneously. Prioritize your goals based on their importance and urgency. Focus on addressing the most critical areas first before moving on to others.

Set Short-term and Long-term Goals:

Break down your recovery journey into manageable steps by setting both short-term and long-term goals.

Short-term goals provide immediate direction and motivation, while long-term goals help you envision your desired outcomes and stay committed to the bigger picture.

Make Your Goals Realistic and Achievable:

Set goals that are realistic and within your reach. Avoid setting yourself up for failure by aiming too high or expecting instant results. Start with small, attainable steps and gradually increase the difficulty as you progress.

Be Flexible and Adaptive:

Recognize that recovery is a dynamic process, and your goals may need to be adjusted along the way.

Be flexible and adaptive in your approach, and don't be discouraged by setbacks or obstacles. Use them as opportunities for learning and growth.

Create a Plan of Action:

Develop a clear plan of action for each goal, outlining the specific steps you need to take to achieve it. Break down larger goals into smaller tasks and establish deadlines to keep yourself accountable.

Seek Support and Accountability:

Share your goals with trusted friends, family members, or professionals who can provide support, encouragement, and accountability.

Consider joining a support group or seeking guidance from a therapist or counselor who specializes in addiction recovery.

Celebrate Your Progress:

Celebrate your achievements and milestones along the way, no matter how small they may seem. Acknowledge the progress you've made and use it as motivation to keep moving forward on your recovery journey.

By setting clear, realistic, and meaningful goals, you empower yourself to take control of your recovery and create positive change in your life.

Remember that recovery is a journey, and setting goals is just the first step toward a brighter, drug-free future.

Building a Support System

Building a strong support system is essential for successful recovery from drug abuse. Here's how you can establish and nurture a supportive network:

Reach Out to Family and Friends:

Start by reaching out to supportive family members and friends who can offer encouragement, understanding, and practical assistance.

Share your struggles and goals with them, and let them know how they can best support you in your recovery journey.

Join a Support Group:

Consider joining a support group such as Alcoholics Anonymous (AA), Narcotics Anonymous (NA), or SMART Recovery.

These groups provide a safe and nonjudgmental environment where you can connect with others who are facing similar challenges, share experiences, and learn from each other's successes and setbacks.

Attend Therapy or Counseling Sessions:

Seek professional support from therapists, counselors, or addiction specialists who can provide individualized guidance and support tailored to your needs.

Therapy sessions can help you explore underlying issues contributing to your drug abuse, develop coping skills, and work through challenges in a supportive and confidential setting.

Engage in Peer Support Networks:

Connect with peers who are also in recovery through online forums, social media groups, or community organizations.

Peer support networks offer valuable opportunities for mutual encouragement, accountability, and camaraderie.

Involve Your Healthcare Team:

Work closely with your healthcare team, including doctors, nurses, and other healthcare professionals, to address any medical issues related to your drug abuse and to develop a comprehensive treatment plan. Your healthcare providers can offer guidance, monitor your progress, and make adjustments to your treatment as needed.

Participate in Recreational and Social Activities:

Engage in recreational and social activities that promote health, wellness, and personal fulfillment.

Join clubs, classes, or hobby groups that align with your interests and values, and use these opportunities to connect with like-minded individuals who support your sobriety.

Utilize Community Resources:

Take advantage of community resources and services available to individuals in recovery, such as sober living homes, vocational training programs, job placement services, and legal assistance. These resources can provide additional support and assistance as you rebuild your life in sobriety.

Communicate Your Needs Clearly:

Be open and honest with your support system about your needs, preferences, and boundaries.

Clearly communicate how others can best support you in your recovery, whether it's through offering encouragement, respecting your sobriety, or helping you navigate challenges.

Stay Connected and Engaged:

Stay connected with your support system regularly, whether it's through in-person meetings, phone calls, text messages, or virtual communication.

Cultivate meaningful relationships built on trust, respect, and mutual support, and prioritize staying engaged with those who uplift and empower you in your recovery journey.

Be a Supportive Presence for Others:

Offer support and encouragement to others who are also on the path to recovery.

By giving back and being a supportive presence for others, you not only strengthen your own recovery but also contribute to the collective healing and resilience of the community.

Bear in mind that building a support system takes time, effort, and vulnerability, but the benefits of having a strong support network are invaluable in maintaining sobriety and achieving long-term success in recovery.

Overcoming Triggers and Cravings

Identifying and avoiding triggers is a crucial aspect of managing cravings and preventing relapse in recovery from drug abuse.

Here's a step-by-step guide on how you can effectively identify and navigate triggers:

Understand What Triggers Are:

Triggers are internal or external cues that evoke strong urges or cravings for drugs.

They can vary from person to person and may include people, places, emotions, situations, thoughts, or sensory experiences associated with past drug use.

Reflect on Past Experiences:

Reflect on your past experiences with drug abuse and identify specific triggers that have led to cravings or relapse in the past.

Pay attention to patterns and common themes, and consider how certain people, places, or situations have influenced your drug use.

Keep a Trigger Journal:

Keep a journal or diary to track your thoughts, feelings, and experiences related to cravings and drug use.

Note down any situations, emotions, or events that trigger cravings, as well as your responses and coping strategies. This can help you identify patterns and gain insight into your triggers over time.

Identify High-Risk Situations:

Identify situations or environments that increase your vulnerability to cravings and relapse.

These may include social gatherings where drugs are present, stressful situations, boredom, loneliness, or times of celebration.

Recognize that certain people, places, or activities may be particularly triggering and plan accordingly.

Learn to Recognize Internal Triggers:

Pay attention to internal triggers, such as negative emotions, stress, anxiety, depression, boredom, or physical discomfort, that may contribute to cravings.

Practice self-awareness and mindfulness techniques to recognize when you're experiencing these emotions and develop healthy coping strategies to manage them effectively.

Develop Coping Skills and Strategies:

Equip yourself with a toolbox of coping skills and strategies to deal with triggers and cravings when they arise.

This may include relaxation techniques (e.g., deep breathing, progressive muscle relaxation), distraction techniques (e.g., engaging in hobbies or activities you enjoy), mindfulness practices (e.g., meditation, yoga), and healthy lifestyle habits (e.g., exercise, nutrition, sleep).

Create a Plan for Avoiding Triggers:

Once you've identified your triggers, develop a proactive plan for avoiding or minimizing exposure to them whenever possible.

This may involve making changes to your daily routine, avoiding certain places or social circles, setting boundaries with toxic relationships, and finding alternative activities to replace drug-related activities.

Seek Support from Your Support System:

Lean on your support system for guidance, encouragement, and accountability in identifying and avoiding triggers.

Share your triggers with trusted friends, family members, or support group members, and ask for their support in navigating challenging situations.

Practice Self-Care and Stress Management:

Prioritize self-care practices and stress management techniques to reduce your overall vulnerability to triggers and cravings.

Make time for activities that promote relaxation, enjoyment, and well-being, such as exercise, hobbies, spending time in nature, and connecting with supportive individuals.

Stay Committed to Your Recovery Goals:

Stay committed to your recovery goals and remind yourself of the reasons why you chose to pursue sobriety. Keep your long-term vision in mind and focus on the positive changes you're making in your life.

Trust in your ability to overcome triggers and cravings, and remember that every small victory brings you closer to lasting recovery.

By taking proactive steps to identify, avoid, and cope with triggers, you empower yourself to manage cravings effectively and stay on track in your recovery journey.

Coping Strategies for Cravings

Coping with cravings is an essential skill in maintaining sobriety and preventing relapse during addiction recovery. Below are some effective coping strategies for managing cravings:

Practice Mindfulness and Deep Breathing:

Engage in mindfulness techniques, such as deep breathing exercises, meditation, or progressive muscle relaxation, to bring your focus to the present moment and calm your mind.

Deep breathing can help reduce anxiety and stress, making it easier to ride out cravings without giving in to them.

Distract Yourself with Healthy Activities:

Redirect your attention away from cravings by engaging in healthy and enjoyable activities.

This could include exercising, going for a walk, listening to music, practicing a hobby, reading a book, or spending time with loved ones.

Choose activities that are rewarding and fulfilling to help shift your focus away from cravings.

Challenge Negative Thoughts:

Challenge any negative thoughts or beliefs that may arise during cravings. Remind yourself of the reasons why you decided to pursue sobriety and the negative consequences of giving in to cravings.

Replace negative thoughts with positive affirmations and reminders of your strength and resilience in overcoming challenges.

Use Visualization Techniques:

Visualize yourself successfully overcoming cravings and maintaining sobriety. Imagine yourself in a calm and peaceful environment, free from the grip of addiction.

Visualization can help reinforce your commitment to recovery and strengthen your resolve to resist cravings.

Reach Out for Support:

Reach out to your support system for encouragement, guidance, and accountability during times of cravings. Share your feelings with trusted friends, family members, or support group members who understand what you're going through and can offer empathy and support. Talking about your cravings can help alleviate their intensity and remind you that you're not alone in your recovery journey.

Practice Self-Care:

Prioritize self-care activities that promote physical, emotional, and mental well-being.

Take care of your body by eating nutritious meals, getting regular exercise, staying hydrated, and getting enough sleep.

Engage in activities that help you relax and reduce stress, such as taking a warm bath, practicing yoga, or spending time in nature.

Use Distraction Techniques:

Employ distraction techniques to redirect your attention away from cravings.

Keep yourself occupied with tasks or activities that require concentration and focus, such as solving puzzles, organizing your surroundings, or working on a creative project.

Keeping your mind engaged can help diminish the intensity of cravings and make them more manageable.

Create a Craving Survival Plan:

Develop a personalized craving survival plan that outlines specific strategies and coping mechanisms you can use when cravings arise. Include a list of healthy activities, supportive contacts, and positive affirmations that you can turn to whenever you're struggling with cravings. Having a plan in place can help you feel more prepared and empowered to face cravings head-on.

Practice Acceptance and Mindfulness:

Accept that cravings are a normal and temporary part of the recovery process, and approach them with mindfulness and nonjudgmental awareness.

Allow yourself to experience cravings without resisting or fighting against them, and observe them with curiosity and detachment.

Recognize that cravings will eventually pass and that you have the strength to overcome them.

Seek Professional Help if Needed:

If you're struggling to cope with cravings despite your best efforts, don't hesitate to seek professional help from a therapist, counselor, or addiction specialist.

Professional support can provide additional guidance, coping skills, and resources to help you manage cravings effectively and stay on track in your recovery journey.

Bear in mind that coping with cravings is a skill that takes practice and persistence.

By incorporating these coping strategies into your daily routine and staying committed to your recovery goals, you can build resilience and overcome cravings without compromising your sobriety.

Avoiding High-Risk Situations

Avoiding high-risk situations is a proactive approach to managing cravings and reducing the likelihood of relapse during addiction recovery. Here's how you can effectively avoid high-risk situations:

Identify High-Risk Situations:

Start by identifying situations, environments, and triggers that increase your vulnerability to cravings and relapse.

These may include places where drugs are readily available, social gatherings where substance use is common, stressful situations, boredom, loneliness, or times of celebration.

Develop Self-Awareness:

Cultivate self-awareness and mindfulness to recognize when you're entering a high-risk situation.

Pay attention to your thoughts, emotions, and physical sensations, and be alert to any signs of craving or temptation. Learning to identify early warning signs can help you take proactive steps to avoid or mitigate high-risk situations.

Modify Your Routine:

Modify your daily routine to minimize exposure to high-risk situations. This may involve making changes to your schedule, avoiding certain places or activities associated with drug use, and establishing new habits and routines that support your sobriety.

Be intentional about structuring your time in a way that reduces opportunities for temptation.

Avoid Triggering People and Places:

Stay away from people, places, or situations that trigger cravings or remind you of past drug use.

This may include old friends who still use drugs, bars or clubs where you used to socialize, or neighborhoods where you purchased drugs.

Surround yourself with supportive and positive influences that reinforce your commitment to sobriety.

Plan Ahead for Challenging Situations:

Anticipate situations that may pose challenges to your sobriety, such as parties, holidays, or stressful events, and plan ahead for how you will navigate them.

Have a strategy in place for coping with cravings and avoiding relapse, whether it's bringing a sober friend with you, practicing relaxation techniques, or leaving the situation altogether if necessary.

Establish Boundaries:

Set clear boundaries with friends, family members, and acquaintances regarding your sobriety and what behaviors are acceptable to you. Communicate your needs and boundaries assertively and consistently, and don't be afraid to distance yourself from individuals who undermine your recovery or pressure you to use drugs.

Engage in Healthy Activities:

Fill your time with healthy and fulfilling activities that support your sobriety and promote overall well-being.

Engage in hobbies, sports, creative pursuits, volunteer work, or educational activities that bring you joy and fulfillment. Having meaningful activities to occupy your time can reduce boredom and minimize the desire to use drugs.

Build a Support Network:

Surround yourself with a strong support network of friends, family members, peers, and professionals who understand your recovery journey and can offer encouragement, guidance, and accountability. Lean on your support system for support during challenging times and reach out for help when you need it.

Practice Assertive Communication:

Practice assertive communication skills to assert your needs and boundaries in social situations.

Be honest and upfront about your sobriety, and politely but firmly decline offers of drugs or invitations to engage in substance use.

Assertive communication can help you navigate peer pressure and maintain your commitment to sobriety.

Stay Committed to Your Recovery Goals:

Stay committed to your recovery goals and remind yourself of the reasons why you chose to pursue sobriety.

Keep your long-term vision in mind and focus on the positive changes you're making in your life. Trust in your ability to overcome high-risk situations and stay true to your values and priorities.

By taking proactive steps to avoid high-risk situations and prioritize your sobriety, you empower yourself to stay on track in your recovery journey and build a healthier, more fulfilling life free from the grip of addiction.

Stress Management Techniques

Stress management techniques are invaluable tools for enhancing recovery from drug abuse by helping individuals cope with stressors in healthy and constructive ways.

The following are some effective stress management techniques that can support your recovery:

Deep Breathing Exercises:

Practice deep breathing exercises to promote relaxation and reduce stress levels. Take slow, deep breaths in through your nose, hold for a few seconds, and then exhale slowly through your mouth. Focus on the sensation of your breath filling your lungs and releasing tension from your body.

Progressive Muscle Relaxation (PMR):

Engage in progressive muscle relaxation to release tension and promote relaxation throughout your body.

Start by tensing and then slowly relaxing each muscle group, starting from your toes and working your way up to your head. Focus on the sensation of tension melting away as you relax each muscle group.

Mindfulness Meditation:

Practice mindfulness meditation to cultivate present-moment awareness and reduce stress reactivity. Set aside time each day to sit quietly and focus on your breath, sensations in your body, or sounds in your environment. Notice any thoughts or emotions that arise without judgment and gently return your attention to the present moment.

Yoga or Tai Chi:

Participate in yoga or tai chi classes to promote relaxation, flexibility, and mindfulness.

These mind-body practices combine physical postures, breathing exercises, and meditation to reduce stress and improve overall well-being.

Choose classes that emphasize gentle movements and relaxation rather than intense exertion.

Exercise Regularly:

Engage in regular physical activity to reduce stress, improve mood, and boost overall health.

Choose activities you enjoy, such as walking, jogging, swimming, cycling, or dancing, and aim for at least 30 minutes of moderate-intensity exercise most days of the week.

Exercise releases endorphins, natural chemicals that promote feelings of happiness and well-being.

Connect with Nature:

Spend time outdoors in nature to reduce stress and promote relaxation. Take walks in the park, hike in the mountains, or simply sit and enjoy the beauty of natural surroundings. Connecting with nature can help you feel grounded, peaceful, and connected to something greater than yourself.

Practice Relaxation Techniques:

Explore relaxation techniques such as guided imagery, visualization, or aromatherapy to reduce stress and promote relaxation.

Picture yourself in a peaceful, serene environment or use calming scents like lavender or chamomile to create a soothing atmosphere.

Maintain a Healthy Lifestyle:

Prioritize self-care activities that promote physical, emotional, and mental well-being. Eat a balanced diet rich in fruits, vegetables, whole grains, and lean proteins, stay hydrated by drinking plenty of water, get adequate sleep each night, and avoid excessive caffeine, nicotine, and alcohol.

Set Boundaries and Prioritize Self-Care:

Establish boundaries to protect your time, energy, and emotional well-being.

Learn to say no to requests or obligations that add unnecessary stress to your life and prioritize activities that replenish and rejuvenate you.

Make self-care a priority by scheduling regular time for relaxation, leisure, and activities that bring you joy.

Seek Professional Support:

If you're struggling to manage stress despite your best efforts, don't hesitate to seek professional support from a therapist, counselor, or support group. Professional support can provide additional guidance, coping strategies, and resources to help you manage stress effectively and maintain your recovery.

Emotion Regulation Strategies

Emotion regulation strategies are vital tools for enhancing recovery from drug abuse by helping individuals manage challenging emotions without turning to substances.

Below are some effective emotion regulation strategies that can support your recovery:

Identify and Label Emotions:

Practice identifying and labeling your emotions accurately. Pay attention to how you're feeling in different situations and give names to your emotions, such as anger, sadness, anxiety, or joy.

Recognizing and acknowledging your emotions is the first step toward effectively regulating them.

Practice Mindfulness:

Engage in mindfulness practices to cultivate present-moment awareness and nonjudgmental acceptance of your emotions.

Set aside time each day to practice mindfulness meditation, mindful breathing, or body scan exercises.

Notice the sensations, thoughts, and emotions that arise without reacting to them, and cultivate an attitude of curiosity and openness.

Use Cognitive Restructuring:

Challenge and reframe negative or irrational thoughts that contribute to distressing emotions.

Practice cognitive restructuring techniques to identify and replace unhelpful thought patterns with more balanced and realistic perspectives.

Ask yourself questions such as, "Is this thought true? Is it helpful? What evidence do I have to support or refute it?"

Develop Coping Skills:

Build a toolbox of healthy coping skills to manage distressing emotions without resorting to drugs. Experiment with different coping strategies, such as deep breathing, relaxation techniques, journaling, creative expression, or physical activity, and identify which ones work best for you in different situations.

Seek Social Support:

Reach out to supportive friends, family members, or peers when you're struggling with difficult emotions.

Share your feelings with trusted individuals who can offer empathy, validation, and perspective.

Social support can provide comfort, reassurance, and a sense of connection during challenging times.

Engage in Self-Care Activities:

Prioritize self-care activities that promote physical, emotional, and mental well-being. Take time to engage in activities you enjoy, such as hobbies, exercise, spending time in nature, or practicing relaxation techniques. Nourish your body with nutritious food, stay hydrated, and get enough restful sleep each night.

Set Boundaries:

Establish clear boundaries to protect your emotional well-being and prevent others from triggering distressing emotions.

Learn to assertively communicate your needs and limits in relationships and situations, and don't be afraid to say no to requests or obligations that add unnecessary stress to your life.

Practice Emotional Regulation Skills:

Develop skills for regulating and expressing emotions effectively. Learn to identify healthy ways of expressing emotions, such as assertive communication, active listening, and problem-solving.

Practice emotional regulation techniques, such as self-soothing, relaxation, and grounding exercises, to manage intense emotions in the moment.

Engage in Therapy or Counseling:

Seek professional support from a therapist, counselor, or support group specializing in addiction recovery and emotion regulation.

Therapy can provide a safe and supportive space to explore underlying emotional issues, learn new coping skills, and develop strategies for managing emotions in healthy ways.

Practice Self-Compassion:

Cultivate self-compassion by treating yourself with kindness, understanding, and acceptance during times of distress.

Offer yourself words of encouragement, validation, and reassurance, and practice self-care rituals that nurture and replenish your emotional well-being.

Incorporating these emotion regulation strategies into your daily life can help enhance your ability to manage challenging emotions and navigate the ups and downs of recovery from drug abuse.

Don't forget that learning to regulate emotions is a skill that takes time and practice, so be patient and gentle with yourself as you continue on your journey of healing and growth.

Building Resilience

Building resilience is essential for enhancing recovery from drug abuse, as it equips individuals with the strength and adaptability to overcome challenges and setbacks along the journey to sobriety.

Here are some strategies for building resilience that can support your recovery:

Cultivate Self-Awareness:

Develop self-awareness by reflecting on your thoughts, emotions, behaviors, and patterns of coping.

Pay attention to your strengths, weaknesses, triggers, and coping mechanisms, and strive to deepen your understanding of yourself and your recovery journey.

Practice Optimism and Positive Thinking:

Cultivate an optimistic mindset by focusing on the positive aspects of your life and recovery.

Challenge negative thoughts and beliefs that undermine your confidence and resilience, and cultivate gratitude for the progress you've made and the support you receive along the way.

Build Strong Social Connections:

Nurture supportive relationships with friends, family members, peers, and professionals who understand and validate your experiences.

Lean on your support network for encouragement, guidance, and empathy during challenging times, and offer support to others in return.

Develop Problem-Solving Skills:

Strengthen your problem-solving skills by approaching challenges and obstacles as opportunities for growth and learning.

Break down problems into manageable steps, brainstorm potential solutions, and take proactive steps to address them.

Seek help and guidance from others when needed, and be willing to adapt and adjust your approach as you go.

Cultivate Flexibility and Adaptability:

Practice flexibility and adaptability by embracing change and uncertainty as natural parts of the recovery process. Be open to trying new approaches, exploring different perspectives, and adjusting your goals and expectations as needed. Cultivate a mindset of resilience that enables you to bounce back from setbacks and setbacks with resilience and determination.

Build Emotional Regulation Skills:

Develop skills for regulating and managing your emotions effectively.

Learn to recognize and label your emotions, practice mindfulness techniques to stay present and grounded, and use healthy coping strategies to cope with stress and distress.

Cultivate self-compassion and self-care rituals that nurture your emotional well-being and resilience.

Set Realistic Goals and Expectations:

Set realistic, achievable goals for yourself that align with your values, priorities, and capabilities.

Break larger goals down into smaller, manageable steps, and celebrate your progress and achievements along the way.

Avoid comparing yourself to others and focus on your own unique journey of recovery and growth.

Practice Self-Care and Well-Being:

Prioritize self-care activities that nourish and replenish your physical, emotional, and mental well-being.

Take time to rest, relax, and recharge, and engage in activities that bring you joy, fulfillment, and peace. Maintain a healthy lifestyle with regular exercise, nutritious food, adequate sleep, and stress management practices.

Seek Professional Support and Guidance:

Don't hesitate to seek professional support and guidance from therapists, counselors, or support groups specializing in addiction recovery and resilience-building.

Therapy can provide a safe and supportive space to explore your experiences, learn new skills, and develop strategies for overcoming challenges and obstacles.

Cultivate Gratitude and Resilience Mindset:

Cultivate gratitude for the blessings and opportunities in your life, even in the face of adversity. Practice reframing setbacks and failures as opportunities for learning and growth, and recognize your own strength, courage, and resilience in overcoming obstacles and moving forward in your recovery journey.

Incorporating these strategies into your daily life can help build resilience and fortify your capacity to overcome challenges, navigate setbacks, and thrive in your recovery from drug abuse.

Self-Compassion and Forgiveness

Practicing self-compassion and forgiveness is crucial for enhancing recovery from drug abuse, as it allows individuals to cultivate kindness, understanding, and acceptance toward themselves, ultimately promoting healing and growth.

Here are some strategies for cultivating self-compassion and forgiveness that can support your recovery:

Practice Mindfulness and Self-Awareness:

Cultivate mindfulness by bringing nonjudgmental awareness to your thoughts, emotions, and sensations in the present moment. Notice any self-critical or judgmental thoughts that arise and observe them with curiosity and compassion.

Develop self-awareness by recognizing patterns of self-criticism and learning to respond to yourself with kindness and understanding.

Cultivate a Compassionate Inner Voice:

Develop a compassionate inner voice that speaks to you with kindness, encouragement, and support.

Challenge self-critical or negative thoughts by offering yourself words of reassurance, validation, and comfort.

Treat yourself with the same compassion and empathy that you would offer to a loved one in a similar situation.

Practice Self-Kindness:

Be gentle and kind to yourself, especially during times of struggle or difficulty. Treat yourself with the same kindness and compassion that you would offer to a friend in need.

Practice self-care activities that nourish and replenish your physical, emotional, and mental well-being, such as taking a warm bath, going for a walk in nature, or spending time with loved ones.

Cultivate Gratitude and Appreciation:

Cultivate gratitude for the blessings and opportunities in your life, even amidst challenges and setbacks.

Take time each day to reflect on the things you're grateful for, whether it's supportive relationships, moments of joy, or personal strengths and accomplishments. Cultivating gratitude can shift your perspective and foster a sense of abundance and contentment.

Release Guilt and Shame:

Release feelings of guilt and shame by acknowledging and accepting mistakes and shortcomings without judgment or self-condemnation.

Recognize that you're human and fallible, and that making mistakes is a natural part of the human experience.

Practice self-compassion by offering yourself forgiveness and understanding, and letting go of any lingering guilt or shame.

Challenge Perfectionism and Self-Criticism:

Challenge perfectionistic tendencies and unrealistic expectations of yourself by embracing imperfection and embracing self-compassion.

Recognize that nobody is perfect, and that striving for perfection only leads to stress, anxiety, and self-criticism.

Embrace your flaws and imperfections as part of what makes you uniquely human, and treat yourself with kindness and acceptance.

Practice Forgiveness Toward Yourself:

Practice forgiveness toward yourself for past mistakes, regrets, and actions taken during active addiction. Acknowledge any harm you may have caused yourself or others, and offer yourself forgiveness and compassion for your past behaviors.

Recognize that forgiveness is a process, and that it's okay to take small steps toward self-forgiveness over time.

Seek Support and Guidance:

Seek support and guidance from therapists, counselors, or support groups specializing in addiction recovery and self-compassion.

Therapy can provide a safe and supportive space to explore feelings of guilt, shame, and self-criticism, and develop strategies for cultivating self-compassion and forgiveness.

Practice Self-Compassion Exercises:

Engage in self-compassion exercises and practices to cultivate kindness and understanding toward yourself. This may include self-compassion meditations, writing compassionate letters to yourself, or practicing loving-kindness meditation directed toward yourself and others.

Be Patient and Gentle with Yourself:

Be patient and gentle with yourself as you navigate the process of self-compassion and forgiveness.

Recognize that healing takes time and effort, and that it's okay to have setbacks or moments of struggle along the way.

Treat yourself with the same patience, kindness, and understanding that you would offer to a dear friend on their journey of healing and growth.

By incorporating these strategies into your recovery journey, you can cultivate self-compassion and forgiveness, promote healing and resilience, and move forward with greater compassion, understanding, and acceptance toward yourself.

Dealing with Setbacks

Dealing with setbacks is an inevitable part of the recovery journey from drug abuse. However, setbacks don't have to derail your progress.

The following are some strategies for effectively dealing with setbacks and maintaining momentum in your recovery:

Acknowledge Your Feelings:

Allow yourself to acknowledge and validate your feelings in response to setbacks. It's natural to feel disappointed, frustrated, or discouraged, but try not to dwell on negative emotions.

Instead, recognize and accept your feelings as valid reactions to the situation.

Practice Self-Compassion:

Be kind and compassionate toward yourself during setbacks. Treat yourself with the same understanding, support, and empathy that you would offer to a friend facing a similar challenge.

Practice self-compassion by acknowledging your efforts and progress, and offering yourself words of encouragement and reassurance.

Reframe Setbacks as Learning Opportunities:

Reframe setbacks as learning opportunities and opportunities for growth. Instead of viewing setbacks as failures, see them as valuable lessons that can help you identify areas for improvement, strengthen your coping skills, and deepen your understanding of yourself and your recovery journey.

Identify Triggers and Underlying Factors:

Take time to reflect on the factors that contributed to the setback and identify any triggers or underlying issues that may have played a role.

This could include stress, emotional distress, social pressure, or lapses in self-care. By understanding the factors that led to the setback, you can develop strategies to address them more effectively in the future.

Reach Out for Support:

Reach out to your support network for guidance, encouragement, and perspective during setbacks. Share your experiences with trusted friends, family members, or support group members who understand your recovery journey and can offer empathy and support.

Don't hesitate to seek professional help if you're struggling to cope with setbacks on your own.

Review and Adjust Your Recovery Plan:

Review your recovery plan and consider whether any adjustments or modifications are needed in light of the setback.

This may involve revisiting your goals, refining your coping strategies, or seeking additional support or resources. Be flexible and willing to adapt your plan as needed to better meet your changing needs and circumstances.

Focus on What You Can Control:

Focus on what you can control rather than dwelling on factors outside of your control.

While you may not be able to change the past or prevent setbacks from occurring, you can take proactive steps to manage your response to them and to strengthen your resilience and coping skills moving forward.

Practice Healthy Coping Strategies:

Engage in healthy coping strategies to manage stress, anxiety, and other emotions that may arise during setbacks.

This could include practicing relaxation techniques, engaging in physical activity, journaling, or seeking support from others. Find activities that help you feel grounded, centered, and supported during challenging times.

Stay Committed to Your Recovery Goals:

Stay committed to your recovery goals and remind yourself of the reasons why you chose to pursue sobriety.

Use setbacks as opportunities to reaffirm your commitment to your recovery journey and to recommit to your goals and values. Trust in your ability to overcome challenges and setbacks with resilience and determination.

Celebrate Progress and Small Victories:

Celebrate your progress and small victories along the way, even in the face of setbacks. Recognize and acknowledge the steps you've taken and the progress you've made, no matter how small. Celebrating progress can boost your confidence, motivation, and sense of accomplishment, helping you stay focused and resilient in your recovery journey.

By implementing these strategies, setbacks can become opportunities for growth, learning, and renewed commitment to your recovery journey.

Remember that setbacks are a natural part of the process, and with perseverance, support, and self-compassion, you can overcome them and continue moving forward toward a healthier, more fulfilling life free from the grip of drug abuse.

Mindfulness Practices for Recovery

Mindfulness practices are powerful tools for recovery from drug abuse, as they help individuals cultivate present-moment awareness, nonjudgmental acceptance, and emotional regulation.

Below are some mindfulness practices specifically tailored for recovery:

Mindful Breathing:

Practice mindful breathing exercises to anchor yourself in the present moment and calm your mind. Sit comfortably in a quiet space and focus your attention on your breath as you inhale and exhale slowly and deeply. Notice the sensations of your breath as it enters and leaves your body, and gently bring your attention back to your breath whenever your mind wanders.

Body Scan Meditation:

Engage in body scan meditation to develop awareness of physical sensations and promote relaxation.

Lie down or sit comfortably and systematically scan your body from head to toe, paying attention to any areas of tension, discomfort, or relaxation.

Notice the sensations in each part of your body without judgment or attachment, and allow yourself to fully experience the present moment.

Sensory Awareness:

Practice sensory awareness exercises to engage your senses and cultivate mindfulness in everyday activities.

Choose an object, such as a piece of fruit or a cup of tea, and explore it with your senses.

Notice its color, texture, scent, taste, and sound, and fully immerse yourself in the sensory experience without judgment or distraction.

Mindful Walking:

Practice mindful walking to bring awareness to the sensations of movement and grounding in your body.

Take a slow, deliberate walk outdoors or indoors, paying attention to each step you take and the sensations of your feet touching the ground. Notice the sights, sounds, and smells around you as you walk, and stay present in the moment.

Mindful Eating:

Practice mindful eating to cultivate awareness and enjoyment of food while reducing impulsive or emotional eating habits.

Take time to savor each bite of your meal or snack, noticing the colors, textures, flavors, and sensations in your mouth. Pay attention to hunger and fullness cues, and eat slowly and mindfully without distractions.

Loving-Kindness Meditation:

Engage in loving-kindness meditation to cultivate compassion and goodwill toward yourself and others. Sit comfortably and silently repeat phrases of loving-kindness, such as "May I be happy, may I be healthy, may I be at peace," directing them toward yourself and then gradually extending them to others. Practice sending feelings of love, kindness, and compassion to yourself and all beings.

Mindful Journaling:

Practice mindful journaling to explore your thoughts, emotions, and experiences with curiosity and nonjudgment. Set aside time each day to write in a journal, focusing on your present-moment experiences and reflections.

Use journaling as a tool for self-discovery, emotional processing, and cultivating mindfulness in your daily life.

Mindful Communication:

Practice mindful communication by listening attentively and speaking intentionally in your interactions with others.

Pay full attention to the speaker without interrupting or formulating a response, and notice your own thoughts, emotions, and body language as you communicate.

Use mindful communication to foster deeper connections, understanding, and empathy in your relationships.

Mindful Relaxation Techniques:

Engage in mindful relaxation techniques, such as progressive muscle relaxation, guided imagery, or deep breathing exercises, to reduce stress and promote relaxation. Set aside time each day to practice relaxation techniques, allowing yourself to unwind and release tension in your body and mind.

Mindfulness in Daily Activities:

Infuse mindfulness into your daily activities by bringing awareness and presence to everything you do.

Whether you're washing dishes, walking the dog, or brushing your teeth, practice being fully engaged in the present moment and noticing the sensations, thoughts, and emotions that arise without judgment or attachment.

By incorporating these mindfulness practices into your recovery journey, you can develop greater self-awareness, emotional regulation, and resilience, and cultivate a deeper sense of connection to yourself and the world around you.

Nutrition for Recovery

Nutrition plays a crucial role in supporting recovery from drug addiction by promoting physical health, stabilizing mood and energy levels, and addressing nutritional deficiencies that may arise during active addiction.

Here's how nutrition can help you recover from drug addiction and the importance of key nutrients:

Supporting Physical Health:

Proper nutrition provides the essential nutrients your body needs to function optimally and repair damage caused by drug abuse. A balanced diet rich in vitamins, minerals, protein, healthy fats, and carbohydrates supports overall physical health, boosts immunity, and enhances energy levels and vitality.

Balancing Mood and Energy Levels:

Nutrition plays a key role in regulating mood and energy levels, which can be disrupted during addiction recovery.

Consuming a balanced diet that includes complex carbohydrates, lean proteins, and healthy fats helps stabilize blood sugar levels and neurotransmitter function, reducing mood swings, cravings, and fatigue.

Supporting Brain Health:

Nutrient-rich foods provide the building blocks necessary for optimal brain function and neurotransmitter production.

Adequate intake of essential nutrients such as omega-3 fatty acids, vitamins B6 and B12, folate, and magnesium supports cognitive function, memory, concentration, and mood regulation, all of which are important for recovery.

Reducing Cravings and Withdrawal Symptoms:

Proper nutrition can help reduce cravings and alleviate withdrawal symptoms associated with drug addiction.

Certain nutrients, such as amino acids, vitamins, and minerals, play a role in neurotransmitter synthesis and regulation, which can help stabilize mood and reduce cravings for drugs or alcohol.

Promoting Physical Healing:

Recovery from drug addiction often involves physical healing and rehabilitation.

Nutrient-dense foods provide the essential nutrients necessary for tissue repair, muscle recovery, and overall physical health, supporting the body's natural healing processes and reducing the risk of complications during recovery.

Enhancing Mental Health and Well-Being:

Good nutrition is essential for mental health and well-being, which are critical aspects of addiction recovery.

Nutrient deficiencies can contribute to symptoms of depression, anxiety, and other mental health disorders, while a balanced diet rich in vitamins, minerals, and antioxidants supports emotional stability, resilience, and overall well-being.

Boosting Energy and Vitality:

Recovery from drug addiction can be physically and emotionally demanding, requiring energy and vitality to sustain long-term sobriety.

Proper nutrition provides the fuel your body needs to maintain energy levels, support physical activity, and engage fully in daily life, helping you feel more energized, resilient, and motivated.

Key Nutrients for Recovery from Drug Addiction and Their Importance:

Protein:

Importance: Supports muscle repair and growth, stabilizes blood sugar levels, and promotes satiety and muscle recovery.

Food Sources: Lean meats, poultry, fish, eggs, dairy products, legumes, nuts, and seeds.

Omega-3 Fatty Acids:

Importance: Supports brain health, cognitive function, mood regulation, and reduces inflammation.

Food Sources: Fatty fish (salmon, mackerel, sardines), flaxseeds, chia seeds, walnuts, and hemp seeds.

Complex Carbohydrates:

Importance: Provides sustained energy, stabilizes blood sugar levels, and supports mood and cognitive function.

Food Sources: Whole grains (brown rice, quinoa, oats), fruits, vegetables, legumes, and beans.

Vitamins B6 and B12:

Importance: Essential for neurotransmitter synthesis, energy metabolism, mood regulation, and cognitive function.

Food Sources: Lean meats, poultry, fish, eggs, dairy products, fortified cereals, legumes, and leafy greens.

Folate (Vitamin B9):

Importance: Supports neurotransmitter synthesis, mood regulation, and cognitive function.

Food Sources: Leafy greens, legumes, avocado, citrus fruits, nuts, seeds, and fortified grains.

Magnesium:

Importance: Supports relaxation, stress management, muscle function, and energy metabolism.

Food Sources: Leafy greens, nuts, seeds, whole grains, legumes, avocado, bananas, and dark chocolate.

Antioxidants (Vitamins C and E):

Importance: Protects against oxidative stress, inflammation, and supports immune function and overall health.

Food Sources: Citrus fruits, berries, bell peppers, tomatoes, nuts, seeds, spinach, and vegetable oils.

Zinc:

Importance: Supports immune function, wound healing, neurotransmitter function, and overall health.

Food Sources: Lean meats, poultry, seafood, nuts, seeds, whole grains, and legumes.

Water:

Importance: Hydrates the body, supports detoxification, regulates body temperature, and promotes overall health and well-being.

Food Sources: Water, herbal teas, fruits, vegetables, and soups.

By prioritizing nutrient-dense foods and incorporating key nutrients into your diet, you can support your recovery from drug addiction, promote physical and emotional well-being, and enhance your overall health and vitality.

Additionally, consulting with a registered dietitian or nutritionist can provide personalized guidance and support to help optimize your nutrition and support your recovery journey.

Exercise as a Tool for Healing

Exercise can play a significant role in aiding recovery from drug addiction by promoting physical health, reducing cravings and withdrawal symptoms, improving mood and mental well-being, and supporting overall recovery efforts.

Here's how exercise can help in recovery, along with some types of exercises and their importance:

Physical Health Benefits:

Exercise promotes physical health by strengthening muscles, improving cardiovascular health, increasing flexibility and mobility, and supporting weight management. Regular exercise can help restore physical health that may have been compromised during active addiction, reducing the risk of chronic diseases and improving overall well-being.

Reduced Cravings and Withdrawal Symptoms:

Engaging in regular exercise has been shown to reduce cravings for drugs or alcohol and alleviate withdrawal symptoms during recovery.

Exercise stimulates the release of endorphins and other neurotransmitters in the brain, producing feelings of pleasure and euphoria that can help reduce cravings and promote a sense of well-being.

Improved Mood and Mental Health:

Exercise has powerful mood-enhancing effects and can help alleviate symptoms of depression, anxiety, and stress, which are common co-occurring disorders in addiction recovery.

Regular physical activity releases neurotransmitters such as serotonin, dopamine, and norepinephrine, which can improve mood, reduce stress, and enhance mental clarity and focus.

Stress Reduction and Coping Skills:

Exercise serves as a healthy outlet for stress and a constructive way to cope with challenging emotions and triggers.

Engaging in physical activity can help reduce tension, promote relaxation, and provide a sense of control and empowerment over one's body and mind. Exercise can also serve as a distraction from cravings and negative thoughts, allowing individuals to focus on positive goals and activities.

Enhanced Self-Esteem and Confidence:

Regular exercise can boost self-esteem and confidence by improving physical fitness, body image, and self-perception.

Achieving fitness goals, building strength and endurance, and experiencing the positive effects of exercise on overall health can enhance feelings of self-worth and accomplishment, supporting recovery efforts and promoting a positive sense of identity.

Increased Energy and Vitality:

Exercise increases energy levels and vitality, helping individuals feel more alert, focused, and motivated in their recovery journey.

Regular physical activity improves circulation, oxygenation, and metabolism, leading to increased energy levels and reduced feelings of fatigue and lethargy commonly experienced during recovery.

Social Support and Connection:

Exercise can provide opportunities for social support and connection, which are essential for recovery from addiction.

Participating in group exercise classes, sports activities, or outdoor adventures allows individuals to connect with others who share similar interests and goals, fostering a sense of community, belonging, and camaraderie.

Types of Exercises for Recovery and Their Importance:

Aerobic Exercise (Cardiovascular Exercise):

Importance: Improves cardiovascular health, boosts mood, reduces stress, and increases energy levels. Examples include walking, jogging, cycling, swimming, dancing, and aerobic fitness classes.

Strength Training (Resistance Exercise):

Importance: Builds muscle strength and endurance, improves metabolism, supports weight management, and enhances overall physical fitness. Examples include weightlifting, bodyweight exercises, resistance band workouts, and circuit training.

Flexibility and Stretching Exercises:

Importance: Increases flexibility, improves range of motion, reduces muscle tension and soreness, and promotes relaxation. Examples include yoga, Pilates, tai chi, and static stretching exercises.

Mind-Body Exercises:

Importance: Integrates physical movement with mindfulness and relaxation techniques, promoting mental clarity, stress reduction, and emotional well-being. Examples include yoga, tai chi, qigong, and mindful movement practices.

Outdoor Activities and Nature-Based Exercise:

Importance: Enhances mood, reduces stress, and promotes a sense of connection to nature and the outdoors. Examples include hiking, trail running, cycling, kayaking, rock climbing, and outdoor sports.

Group Exercise Classes and Team Sports:

Importance: Provides social support, accountability, and camaraderie, fostering a sense of community and connection with others.

Examples include group fitness classes, team sports (e.g., soccer, basketball, volleyball), and recreational leagues.

Mindful Movement and Meditation Practices:

Importance: Combines physical movement with mindfulness and meditation techniques to promote relaxation, stress reduction, and emotional well-being.

Examples include mindful walking, walking meditation, and mindful movement practices.

Incorporating a variety of exercises into your daily routine can help you reap the full benefits of physical activity and support your recovery from drug addiction.

Remember to start slowly and gradually increase intensity and duration as your fitness level improves, and always consult with a healthcare professional before starting any new exercise program, especially if you have any underlying health conditions or concerns.

By making exercise a regular part of your recovery journey, you can enhance your physical and mental well-being, reduce cravings and withdrawal symptoms, and build a foundation for a healthy, fulfilling life in sobriety.

Creating a Healthy Lifestyle Routine

Creating a healthy lifestyle routine is essential for supporting your recovery from drug addiction and promoting overall well-being.

A well-rounded routine encompasses various aspects of physical, mental, and emotional health, including nutrition, exercise, sleep, stress management, self-care, and social connection.

Here's a guide to creating a healthy lifestyle routine to support your recovery:

Establish a Consistent Daily Schedule:

Set a regular daily schedule that includes consistent wake-up and bedtime hours, meal times, exercise sessions, and self-care activities.

Consistency helps regulate your body's internal clock, promotes better sleep, and provides structure and stability to your day.

Prioritize Nutrition and Hydration:

Focus on consuming a balanced diet rich in fruits, vegetables, whole grains, lean proteins, and healthy fats. Aim to eat regular, nutritious meals and stay hydrated by drinking plenty of water throughout the day.

Avoid processed foods, sugary snacks, and excessive caffeine and alcohol, which can disrupt energy levels and mood.

Incorporate Regular Exercise:

Include regular exercise and physical activity in your routine to promote physical health, reduce stress, and enhance mood.

Choose activities you enjoy, such as walking, jogging, cycling, swimming, yoga, or strength training, and aim for at least 30 minutes of moderate-intensity exercise most days of the week.

Practice Stress Management Techniques:

Incorporate stress management techniques into your daily routine to reduce stress and promote relaxation. This may include mindfulness meditation, deep breathing exercises, progressive muscle relaxation, yoga, tai chi, or spending time in nature. Find activities that help you unwind and recharge, and prioritize them regularly.

Ensure Sufficient Sleep:

Prioritize getting adequate sleep each night to support physical and mental health. Aim for 7-9 hours of quality sleep per night and establish a relaxing bedtime routine to promote better sleep hygiene.

Create a comfortable sleep environment, limit screen time before bed, and avoid caffeine and heavy meals close to bedtime.

Engage in Self-Care Activities:

Make time for self-care activities that nurture your physical, mental, and emotional well-being. This may include practicing hobbies, spending time with loved ones, reading, journaling, taking baths, or engaging in creative pursuits. Listen to your needs and prioritize activities that replenish your energy and bring you joy and fulfillment.

Build Supportive Relationships:

Cultivate supportive relationships with friends, family members, peers, and professionals who understand and validate your experiences.

Lean on your support network for encouragement, guidance, and empathy during challenging times, and offer support to others in return.

Foster meaningful connections that contribute to your sense of belonging and community.

Set Boundaries and Practice Self-Compassion:

Set boundaries to protect your physical and emotional well-being and prioritize self-care.

Learn to say no to activities or obligations that drain your energy or compromise your recovery efforts, and practice self-compassion and self-acceptance.

Treat yourself with kindness, understanding, and forgiveness, especially during times of struggle or setback.

Seek Professional Support and Guidance:

Don't hesitate to seek professional support and guidance from therapists, counselors, or support groups specializing in addiction recovery and mental health. Therapy can provide a safe and supportive space to explore your experiences, learn coping skills, and develop strategies for maintaining a healthy lifestyle in recovery.

Stay Flexible and Adaptive:

Stay flexible and adaptive in your approach to creating a healthy lifestyle routine, recognizing that your needs and circumstances may change over time.

Be willing to adjust your routine as needed to accommodate new challenges, opportunities, or priorities, and remain open to trying new activities or strategies that support your recovery and well-being.

By incorporating these elements into your daily life, you can create a healthy lifestyle routine that supports your recovery from drug addiction and promotes overall health and well-being.

Remember that recovery is a journey, and it's okay to seek support and make adjustments along the way as you navigate the ups and downs of the recovery process.

Stay committed to prioritizing your health and well-being, and celebrate the progress you make toward living a fulfilling and sober life.

Understanding Relapse

Understanding relapse is crucial for individuals in recovery from drug addiction, as it helps identify potential triggers, develop coping strategies, and prevent future relapses.

Relapse refers to the return to drug use or addictive behaviors after a period of abstinence or recovery.

It's important to recognize that relapse is a common and often predictable aspect of the recovery process, and it does not signify failure or weakness.

Instead, relapse should be viewed as an opportunity for learning, growth, and renewed commitment to recovery. Here are key aspects to understand about relapse:

Stages of Relapse:

Relapse typically occurs in three stages: emotional relapse, mental relapse, and physical relapse.

Emotional relapse involves experiencing negative emotions and behaviors that can eventually lead to drug use, such as denial, isolation, and mood swings.

Mental relapse involves thoughts and cravings for drugs, as well as ambivalence about recovery.

Physical relapse occurs when a person returns to drug use or addictive behaviors.

Triggers and Warning Signs:

Relapse triggers are situations, emotions, or thoughts that increase the risk of returning to drug use or addictive behaviors.

Common triggers include stress, negative emotions, interpersonal conflicts, exposure to drugs or alcohol, social pressure, and environmental cues associated with past drug use.

It's important to recognize warning signs of relapse, such as cravings, withdrawal symptoms, mood changes, changes in behavior or routine, and thoughts of using drugs.

High-Risk Situations:

High-risk situations are circumstances or environments where the risk of relapse is heightened.

These may include social events where alcohol or drugs are present, being around people who use drugs, experiencing stress or trauma, facing major life changes or challenges, and encountering reminders of past drug use.

Identifying high-risk situations and developing coping strategies to manage them can help prevent relapse.

Learning from Relapse:

Relapse can be a valuable learning experience that provides insights into underlying triggers, vulnerabilities, and areas for growth. It's important to reflect on the circumstances leading up to relapse, identify patterns or warning signs, and develop strategies to prevent future relapses.

Use relapse as an opportunity to reassess your recovery plan, strengthen coping skills, and renew your commitment to sobriety and well-being.

Understanding relapse as a potential part of the recovery journey can empower individuals to take proactive steps to prevent relapse and maintain long-term sobriety.

By recognizing triggers, developing coping skills, seeking support, and learning from relapse experiences, individuals can navigate the challenges of recovery with resilience, self-awareness, and determination.

Relapse Prevention Techniques

Relapse prevention techniques are strategies and tools designed to help individuals in recovery from drug addiction identify, manage, and mitigate the risk of relapse.

These techniques aim to strengthen coping skills, address underlying triggers and vulnerabilities, and promote long-term sobriety and well-being.

Below are some effective relapse prevention techniques:

Identify and Avoid Triggers:

Recognize and avoid situations, people, places, or activities that may trigger cravings or thoughts of drug use.

Common triggers include stress, negative emotions, interpersonal conflicts, exposure to drugs or alcohol, social pressure, and environmental cues associated with past drug use.

Develop Coping Skills:

Learn and practice healthy coping skills to manage cravings, stress, and negative emotions without resorting to drug use.

This may include mindfulness meditation, deep breathing exercises, progressive muscle relaxation, yoga, journaling, engaging in hobbies or activities, and seeking support from others.

Create a Support Network:

Build a strong support network of friends, family members, peers in recovery, sponsors, therapists, counselors, or support groups who understand and validate your experiences.

Lean on your support network for encouragement, guidance, accountability, and empathy during challenging times.

Attend Therapy or Support Groups:

Participate in therapy, counseling, or support groups specializing in addiction recovery to gain insights, tools, and strategies for relapse prevention.

Therapy can help address underlying issues, trauma, or co-occurring disorders that may contribute to addiction and relapse, while support groups provide camaraderie, understanding, and encouragement from peers in similar situations.

Develop Healthy Habits:

Cultivate a healthy lifestyle that supports recovery and well-being. This includes prioritizing nutrition, exercise, sleep, stress management, self-care, and social connection.

Establishing a balanced routine and engaging in activities that promote physical, mental, and emotional health can reduce the risk of relapse and enhance overall quality of life.

Practice Mindfulness and Self-Awareness:

Cultivate mindfulness and self-awareness to become more attuned to your thoughts, emotions, and behaviors.

Mindfulness practices such as meditation, mindful breathing, and body scan exercises can help increase present-moment awareness, reduce impulsivity, and enhance emotional regulation, making it easier to recognize and respond to potential triggers or cravings.

Develop a Relapse Prevention Plan:

Create a relapse prevention plan that outlines specific strategies, coping skills, and resources to help you navigate high-risk situations and prevent relapse. Include triggers, warning signs, coping strategies, emergency contacts, and steps to take if you experience cravings or thoughts of relapse. Review and update your plan regularly to reflect changes in your recovery journey.

Practice Self-Care and Stress Management:

Prioritize self-care activities that nurture your physical, mental, and emotional well-being.

This may include practicing relaxation techniques, engaging in hobbies or activities you enjoy, spending time in nature, getting regular exercise, eating nutritious meals, getting enough sleep, and setting boundaries to protect your health and recovery.

Stay Committed to Recovery:

Stay committed to your recovery journey and take proactive steps to maintain sobriety and well-being.

This may involve attending regular therapy or support group meetings, staying accountable to your support network, practicing healthy habits, and seeking help when needed.

Remember that recovery is a lifelong process, and it's okay to ask for support and guidance along the way.

Learn from Relapse Experiences:

If you experience a relapse, use it as an opportunity for learning and growth. Reflect on the circumstances leading up to the relapse, identify triggers or vulnerabilities, and develop strategies to prevent future relapses. Seek support from your support network and professionals, and renew your commitment to recovery with self-compassion and determination.

Celebrate Your Progress:

Celebrate your progress and achievements in your recovery journey, no matter how small. Recognize and acknowledge your efforts and accomplishments, and be proud of the positive changes you've made in your life.

Celebrating your progress can help boost your motivation and confidence in your ability to stay sober and overcome challenges.

Be Kind to Yourself:

Practice self-compassion and kindness towards yourself, especially during difficult times or setbacks.

Be patient and understanding with yourself, and remember that recovery is a journey with ups and downs.

Treat yourself with the same compassion and empathy you would offer to a friend facing similar challenges.

Creating a relapse prevention plan empowers you to take control of your recovery journey and build a strong foundation for long-term sobriety and well-being.

By identifying triggers, developing coping strategies, building a support network, and staying committed to your recovery goals, you can minimize the risk of relapse and live a fulfilling life free from the grip of addiction.

Strategies for Staying on Track

Staying on track in your recovery journey requires dedication, commitment, and a proactive approach to maintaining sobriety and overall well-being.

Below are some strategies to help you stay on track and navigate the challenges of recovery effectively:

Set Clear and Achievable Goals:

Define clear and achievable goals for your recovery journey, such as maintaining sobriety, improving your physical and mental health, rebuilding relationships, pursuing education or career goals, or engaging in meaningful activities.

Break down larger goals into smaller, manageable steps to make progress more attainable and measurable.

Create a Daily Routine:

Establish a structured daily routine that includes activities and habits that support your recovery and well-being.

Set regular wake-up and bedtime hours, meal times, exercise sessions, self-care activities, and relaxation techniques.

Having a routine provides stability, predictability, and a sense of purpose in your day-to-day life.

Stay Connected to Your Support Network:

Build and maintain a strong support network of friends, family members, peers in recovery, sponsors, therapists, counselors, or support groups who understand and support your recovery goals.

Stay connected to your support network through regular communication, meetings, or gatherings, and reach out for help or guidance when needed.

Manage Stress Effectively:

Develop healthy stress management techniques to cope with stressors and challenges in your life without resorting to drug use.

Practice mindfulness meditation, deep breathing exercises, progressive muscle relaxation, yoga, or journaling to reduce stress and promote relaxation. Identify and address sources of stress in your life proactively, and seek support from others when needed.

Avoid Triggers and High-Risk Situations:

Identify and avoid triggers and high-risk situations that may increase the risk of relapse.

This may include avoiding people, places, or activities associated with past drug use, setting boundaries with individuals who may undermine your recovery, and developing alternative coping strategies for managing cravings or urges.

Stay Educated and Informed:

Stay informed about addiction, recovery, and mental health by seeking out reliable sources of information, attending educational workshops or seminars, reading books or articles on recovery-related topics, and staying connected to professionals or experts in the field.

Knowledge empowers you to make informed decisions and take proactive steps in your recovery journey.

Practice Mindfulness and Self-Awareness:

Cultivate mindfulness and self-awareness to become more attuned to your thoughts, emotions, and behaviors.

Practice mindfulness techniques such as meditation, mindful breathing, or body scan exercises to increase present-moment awareness and reduce impulsivity.

Pay attention to your internal cues and reactions, and respond to them with intention and clarity.

Celebrate Milestones and Progress:

Celebrate your milestones, achievements, and progress in your recovery journey, no matter how small.

Recognize and acknowledge your efforts and accomplishments, and celebrate the positive changes you've made in your life.

Celebrating milestones boosts motivation and reinforces your commitment to sobriety and well-being.

Seek Help When Needed:

Don't hesitate to seek help or support from professionals, peers, or loved ones if you're struggling with cravings, urges, or challenges in your recovery journey. Reach out to therapists, counselors, or support groups for guidance, encouragement, and resources.

Asking for help is a sign of strength and demonstrates your commitment to staying on track with your recovery goals.

Rebuilding Relationships and Restoring Trust

Rebuilding relationships and restoring trust in the aftermath of addiction can be a challenging but rewarding process.

It requires patience, commitment, and open communication from all parties involved. Here are some strategies to help you rebuild relationships and restore trust:

Take Responsibility for Your Actions:

Acknowledge the impact of your addiction on your relationships and take responsibility for any hurt or harm caused. Offer genuine apologies and express remorse for past behavior, demonstrating your willingness to make amends and rebuild trust.

Be Honest and Transparent:

Practice honesty and transparency in your interactions with others. Be open about your struggles, progress, and intentions in recovery, and avoid hiding or minimizing the truth.

Transparency builds trust and fosters authentic connections with loved ones.

Listen Actively and Empathetically:

Practice active listening and empathy when engaging with loved ones.

Validate their feelings, concerns, and experiences without judgment, and demonstrate your willingness to understand their perspective.

Listening attentively shows that you value their emotions and opinions.

Communicate Effectively:

Improve communication skills by expressing yourself clearly, assertively, and respectfully. Use "I" statements to convey your thoughts and feelings without blaming or criticizing others.

Be receptive to feedback and willing to address conflicts or misunderstandings in a constructive manner.

Set Boundaries and Respect Boundaries:

Establish healthy boundaries in your relationships to protect your well-being and maintain sobriety.

Communicate your needs, limits, and expectations clearly and assertively, and respect the boundaries of others. Boundaries create a sense of safety and trust in relationships.

Demonstrate Consistency and Reliability:

Demonstrate consistency and reliability in your words and actions to rebuild trust over time. Follow through on commitments, honor agreements, and show up for loved ones consistently.

Consistency builds confidence and reliability in your character.

Rebuild Trust Through Actions:

Rebuild trust gradually through consistent, trustworthy behavior. Demonstrate integrity, accountability, and reliability in all aspects of your life, including your recovery efforts, personal responsibilities, and relationships.

Trust is earned through actions, not words alone.

Be Patient and Understanding:

Be patient and understanding with yourself and others as you navigate the process of rebuilding relationships and restoring trust.

Recognize that healing takes time and requires effort from all parties involved. Practice self-compassion and empathy towards yourself and loved ones.

Seek Support and Guidance:

Seek support and guidance from therapists, counselors, or support groups specializing in addiction recovery and family therapy. Professional help can provide insights, tools, and strategies for rebuilding relationships, resolving conflicts, and fostering healthy communication patterns.

Celebrate Progress and Milestones:

Celebrate progress and milestones in your journey of rebuilding relationships and restoring trust.

Acknowledge the positive changes you've made, no matter how small, and express gratitude for the support and understanding of loved ones.

Celebrating progress reinforces motivation and strengthens bonds with others.

Rebuilding relationships and restoring trust after addiction requires time, effort, and commitment from all parties involved. By practicing honesty, empathy, effective communication, and consistency in your actions, you can rebuild trust gradually and cultivate meaningful connections with loved ones.

Bear in mind that every step forward, no matter how small, contributes to the healing process and strengthens relationships in the long run.

Rediscovering Passions and Interests

Rediscovering passions and interests is an enriching aspect of the recovery journey from addiction.

It provides an opportunity to reconnect with activities and pursuits that bring joy, fulfillment, and a sense of purpose. Here are some strategies to help you rediscover your passions and interests:

Reflect on Past Hobbies and Interests:

Take time to reflect on hobbies, interests, and activities you enjoyed before addiction took hold.

Consider activities you were passionate about as a child or teenager, as well as hobbies you may have set aside due to the demands of addiction. Reflecting on past interests can provide inspiration for rediscovery.

Try New Activities:

Be open to trying new activities and experiences that pique your curiosity or interest.

Explore a wide range of hobbies, sports, arts, crafts, music, or recreational activities to discover what resonates with you. Keep an open mind and embrace the opportunity for exploration and growth.

Start Small and Build Momentum:

Start small by incorporating simple, manageable activities into your daily routine. Break down larger goals into smaller, achievable steps, and gradually build momentum as you explore new interests. Celebrate your progress and accomplishments along the way, no matter how small.

Follow Your Curiosity:

Follow your curiosity and intuition when exploring new interests. Pay attention to activities or topics that capture your attention or spark excitement, and pursue them further.

Trust your instincts and allow yourself the freedom to explore without judgment or expectation.

Engage in Creative Expression:

Engage in creative forms of expression, such as writing, drawing, painting, music, or dance, to reconnect with your inner creativity and self-expression. Creative activities can serve as outlets for emotions, thoughts, and experiences, fostering healing and self-discovery.

Connect with Nature:

Spend time outdoors in nature to reconnect with the natural world and experience its beauty and serenity.

Take walks in the park, go hiking, camping, gardening, or stargazing, and immerse yourself in the sights, sounds, and sensations of the outdoors. Nature can be a source of inspiration and renewal.

Join Clubs or Groups:

Join clubs, groups, or organizations related to your interests to connect with like-minded individuals and cultivate a sense of community. Attend meetups, workshops, classes, or events focused on topics that interest you, and engage in shared activities and discussions with others.

Volunteer or Give Back:

Volunteer your time and skills to causes or organizations that align with your values and interests.

Giving back to others can provide a sense of purpose, fulfillment, and connection to your community.

Look for volunteer opportunities that allow you to make a positive impact and contribute to meaningful causes.

Be Patient and Persistent:

Be patient and persistent in your pursuit of rediscovering passions and interests.

Understand that it may take time to find activities that resonate with you and bring you joy.

Stay committed to the process of exploration and discovery, and trust that the journey itself is valuable.

Rediscovering passions and interests is a personal and empowering journey that can enrich your life and contribute to your overall well-being in recovery.

By embracing curiosity, creativity, and exploration, you can reconnect with activities that bring joy, fulfillment, and meaning to your life, fostering a sense of purpose and vitality on your journey of recovery.

Conclusion

Throughout this book, we have explored a myriad of strategies, techniques, and insights aimed at empowering individuals to overcome addiction, prevent relapse, and cultivate a fulfilling life of sobriety.

From understanding the science behind addiction to developing coping skills, setting goals, building support systems, and embracing self-compassion, this book provides a roadmap for recovery that is both practical and empowering.

It emphasizes the importance of self-awareness, resilience, and commitment in the face of challenges, while also celebrating the progress and achievements along the way.

By incorporating evidence-based approaches, such as cognitive-behavioral techniques, mindfulness practices, and holistic wellness strategies, readers are equipped with a versatile toolkit for navigating the complexities of addiction recovery.

Through reflection, introspection, and action, individuals are encouraged to tap into their inherent strengths and resources to reclaim their lives and pursue their aspirations with renewed vitality.

As we close this chapter, let us remember that recovery is not a linear journey, but rather a dynamic process of growth, learning, and transformation. It requires courage, perseverance, and a willingness to embrace change. Above all, it requires hope—the belief that a life of health, happiness, and fulfillment is not only possible but within reach.

May this book serve as a beacon of hope and inspiration for all those embarking on the path of addiction recovery.

May it empower individuals to harness their resilience, cultivate their strengths, and embrace a future filled with possibility.

With dedication, support, and the right tools at their disposal, individuals can indeed achieve lasting sobriety and embark on a life of purpose, meaning, and joy.

Printed in the USA
CPSIA information can be obtained
at www.ICGtesting.com
LVHW090903081224
798622LV00008B/77